D0560921

With love
from

_____

to

_____

LITTLE ☆ STARS™

CAPRICORN

A parent's guide to the little star of the family

JOHN ASTROP

with illustrations by the author

ELEMENT

Shaftesbury, Dorset ● Rockport, Massachusetts
Brisbane, Queensland

Published in Great Britain in 1994 by
Element Books Ltd.
Longmead, Shaftesbury, Dorset

Published in the USA in 1994 by
Element, Inc.
42 Broadway, Rockport, MA 01966

Published in Australia in 1994 by
Element Books Ltd.
for Jacaranda Wiley Ltd.
33 Park Road, Milton, Brisbane, 4064

Printed and bound in Great Britain by
BPC Paulton Books Ltd.

British Library Cataloguing in Publication
data available

Library of Congress Cataloguing in publication
data available

ISBN 1-85230-546-0

CONTENTS

The Twelve Signs

Everyone knows a little about the twelve sun signs. It's the easiest way to approach real astrology without going to the trouble of casting up a chart for the exact time of birth. You won't learn everything about a person with the sun sign but you'll know a lot more than if you just use observation and guesswork. The sun is in roughly the same sign and degree of the zodiac at the same time every year. It's a nice astronomical event that doesn't need calculating. So if you're born between

May 22 and June 21 you'll be pretty sure you're a Gemini; between June 22 and July 23 then you're a Cancer and so on. Many people say how can you divide the human race into twelve sections and are there only twelve different types. Well for a start most people make assessments and judgements on their fellow humans with far smaller groups than that. Rich and poor, educated and non-educated, town girl, country boy, etc. Even with these very simple pigeon holes we can combine to make 'Rich educated town boy' and 'poor non-educated country girl'. We try to get as much information as we can about the others that we make relationships with through life. Astrology as a way of describing and understanding others is unsurpassed. Take the traditional meaning of the twelve signs:

Aries - is self-assertive, brave, energetic and pioneering.

Taurus - is careful, possessive, values material things, is able to build and make things grow.

Gemini - is bright-minded, curious, communicative and versatile.

Cancer - is sensitive, family orientated, protective and caring.

Leo - is creative, dramatic, a leader, showy and generous.

Virgo - is organised, critical, perfectionist and practical.

Libra - is balanced, diplomatic, harmonious, sociable, and likes beautiful things.

Scorpio - is strong-willed, magnetic, powerful, extreme, determined and recuperative.

Sagittarius - is adventurous, philosophical, far-thinking, blunt, truth-seeking.

Capricorn - is cautious, responsible, patient, persistent and ambitious.

Aquarius - is rebellious, unorthodox, humanitarian, idealistic, a fighter of good causes.

Pisces - is sensitive, imaginative, caring, visionary and sacrificing.

If you can find anyone in your circle of friends and acquaintances who isn't described pretty neatly by one of the above it would be surprising. Put the twelve signs into different lives and occupations and you see how it works. A Taurean priest would be more likely to devote his life to looking after the physical and material needs of his church members, feeding the poor, setting up charities. A Virgoan bank robber would plan meticulously and never commit spontaneous crimes. A Leo teacher would make learning an entertainment and a pleasure for her pupils.

So with parents and children. A Capricorn child handles the business of growing up and learning in a very different way to a Libran child. A Scorpio parent manages the family quite differently to an Aquarian. The old boast, 'I'm very fair, I treat all my children the same', may not be the best way to help your little ones at all. Our individual drive is the key to making a success of life. The time when we need the most acceptance of the way we are is in childhood. As a parent it's good to know the ways in which our little ones are like us but we must never forget the ways in which they are different.

LITTLE CAPRICORN

Get out the ruled paper, pens, rulers, stop watch and calculator, and start working out a neat smooth-running system for the entire family. Try a few dummy runs just to make sure everything is working well. Ready? OK little Capricorn, you can come in! Yes, you've just acquired the little pillar of your small society. What a delight to any family a child who behaves, a child who respects elders and a child whose purpose in life is to get on! This is the one member of the zodiac that does things in reverse, entering this world with a built in grown-upness that gets progressively younger and younger as the years go by! Ambition is strong in these little characters but nevertheless realistic, setting their sights on what they know they can achieve. Right from the earliest days you will find your tiny Goat sitting by herself, little frown on face, patiently working at something you'd have to pressurise any other child to get on with. Learning is a pleasure for this little realist for each new phase mastered gives more control, and Capricornians love to be in control. Small Goats have come into this world to make their mark and just as soon as they are able they will

want to become a useful working member of the family. Later in life they will find their place working conscientiously if not prominently in the community but just for now they'll settle for helping Mom or Dad. The make believe games that they play will all have a strong realistic element and a toy dustpan and brush will usually be preferred to a book of fairy tales. They play shops, schools but most of all being Mom and Dad. Almost more than any other child, they look up to, and model themselves on, their loving parents. A lot of the others do just the opposite, rebelling against the previous generation in order to find themselves. Little Capricorns, when they see that something works smoothly, do all they can to support and maintain it and for this reason become great traditionalists. This influences their thoroughness in making sure that they have fully understood and become familiar with each phase of learning before they move on to the next one. Great as it is to have such a responsible little one, it would be worrying if there was no childish fun to add to the character, and left to their own devices they do become just a little dull. As their example you'll find it necessary to let your own hair down frequently just to let your little one know it's OK for adults to have fun. Then you'll have the surprise of your life to find you have a comedian in the family. Not just an everyday giggler but a zany, quite eccentric, kind of humour that will enrich your family with its hopefully frequent appearances. You could get lucky and have a budding Mack Sennett, Kenny Everett or Victor Borge.

THE BABY

What is this tiny babe doing with a frown on her face? Only trying to get those little peepers to focus so that she can see where she is and what's going on. Once that is taken in and the routine understood these tiniest of Kids do everything just as they should: bottles are finished, wind relieved, off to sleep, not much trouble at all. Well at least

most of the time. Serious as these little ones always seem to look (often much older than their years), once you respond well to a smile this will be noted and become a regular part of the repertoire. Right from the start little Capricorns look and listen just to find out what is expected of them and in the quiet moments you'll see that serious look on the little face and know that it's 'taking in' time. Slow to move into any fresh activity or phase, once ready, everything is accomplished with extreme patience, never giving up until the desired end is achieved. It will be a delight to see your cautious little one exploring the shape of a spoon until he has completely understood the reason for its shape and has tried out several ways of holding it, decided which is the most secure and efficient way and, only then, carefully and cleanly begin to feed himself.

THE FIRST THREE YEARS

When the slow process of feeling absolutely secure about heaving oneself around on hands and knees is managed, the next phase of getting up on two legs is, although still cautious, more speedily achieved. Once able to emulate those two ideals, Mum and Dad, trotting around like a small shadow, your little one will seek to carefully and accurately imitate whatever you do. If this puts little Capricorn in the mischievous bracket, it's only because he really wants to be a grown-up as soon as possible. Suffer the attempts to use eyeliner and blusher or devise a new filing system for the papers in Dad's briefcase. It wasn't meant to be naughty, just another couple of steps on towards that most desired of achievements, adulthood. With little Capricorn's love of regularity in all things, potty training should be no problem. Your little one rarely gets caught short or taken by surprise about anything, let alone a matter where comfort is concerned. Don't forget to give a little praise though, when the great event arrives. It's sad, but once you get used to how good they are, these little paragons can get taken for granted. Always modest, they rarely show off as do other children, preferring a laid back, more grown-up attitude towards their achievements. Learning  about letters, colours and numbers will be a delight for them and toys and games where you can test their knowledge on these subjects will be much loved with requests for repeat performances. Little Goats, though never boastful, love to show how much they have learned which is why later on they do so well at school.

THE KINDERGARTEN

The first few visits to nursery school will not evoke a great enthusiastic response. Initially the long process of getting used to a change and feeling comfortable about it takes precedence over the novelty of a new social situation. Always looking to the heights, the little mountain Goat will then be more interested in the teachers than the other pupils. Watching and taking in what is expected of her and doing what she feels is correct will have to be dealt with before becoming a really active member of the class. From then on, your little one

can be an example to the rougher, more boisterous elements of the class, from time to time, quite firmly, sorting out minor differences and calming down chaotic situations. It is surprising how this cautious child can modestly but confidently take a leading position when the situation demands.

School and Onwards

Again the transition from kindergarten to school will need a slow but sure understanding of the way things run before any real commitment is shown. This may take some time for although you'd expect your little Capricorn, lover of routine and organised system, to take to school like a duck to water, Capricorns just don't jump into anything without thorough testing. Once the system is worked out and the pecking orders are observed, your little Goat will settle down to become one of the hardest work-

ing members of the class. Never fast, they won't fall into the whizzkid category, showing great bursts of brilliance, but they work steadily and conscientiously towards good end of term results. Always popular, and enjoying a good social life, little Capricorn will be attracted to like minds as friends, feeling more comfortable with other small realists in preference to the more adventurous and reckless members of the class. Knowing well both their abilities and limitations, bigger Capricorns move from school into adult life with a great sense of direction and a knowledge of where they want to be in the future.

THE THREE DIFFERENT
TYPES OF CAPRICORN

THE DECANATES

Astrology traditionally divides each of the signs into three equal parts of ten degrees called the decanates. These give a slightly different quality to the sign depending on whether the child is born in the first, second or third ten days of the thirty-day period when one is in a sign. Each third is ruled by one of the three signs in the same element. Capricorn is an Earth sign and the three Earth signs are Capricorn, Taurus and Virgo. The nature of Earth signs is basically practical so the following three types each has a different way of expressing their practical abilities.

First Decanate - Dec. 22 to Dec. 31

This is the part of Capricorn that is most typical of the sign qualities. Capricorn is an achiever. Never content to stay in a rut, there is a constant need to improve and develop towards some well-defined aim. Little Capricorns from this decanate are steady and sure-footed, never taking a step that they haven't planned. The need for financial security is very strong and they do not like to be dependent on others in this area. As youngsters they already know the value of money and, unlike most other children, learn quickly to save and make it grow. The Capricornian patience invented the phrase 'Look after the pennies and the pounds will look after themselves'. A few, but only a few, get quite eccentric with their riches. Howard Hughes is an extreme example. Generally the 'old when they're young and young when they're old' pattern is pronounced in the first decanate Capricorns. Marlene Dietrich was a very beautiful entertainer in her seventies and still seeming like a woman half her years. At eighty, Matisse was creating beautiful paintings with the verve and colours of an uninhibited child.

Second Decanate - Jan. 1 to Jan. 10

This is the Romantic Achiever, sharing some of the qualities of Taurus and ruled by Venus. The obstinacy of the Bull combined with the persistence of the Goat is an invincible mix of qualities that takes these characters right to the top of their professions. Not all have the same high aims and not all of them are materialistic but wherever they want to go, they get there. Children of this part of the sign usually have pleasant voices and there are many, many, examples of great singers born during this time. Although they still have a strong feeling for the value of money these Capricorns are less frugal with themselves and those around them, acquiring things of great comfort and aesthetic pleasure. Beauty is an important part of their lives and they will build lovely secure homes in romantic places to keep the harsh old world outside. Gracie Fields moved from her plain North country background to the beautiful Isle of Capri. Elvis's Gracelands was almost a fortress to protect him from the public gaze and is now a shrine to his memory.

Third Decanate - Jan. 11 to Jan. 20

These are the Perfectionist Achievers. The combination of the planet Mercury and the sign

Virgo gives a strong desire to clean up the messy old world around them. Always great organisers and usually achieving a place where they can do something to change the chaos that they see, these Capricorns make a strong impact on other people's lives. The Virgoan ability to see the faults and the Capricornian's to make the changes, no matter how long it takes, produces many really outstanding humanitarians who devote their lives to a cause. Joan of Arc, Albert Schweitzer, Martin Luther King, we all know, but many others have quietly worked to improve the world with less recognition. There are a surprising number of saints born under the sign of Capricorn. There are, however, a few sinners too. The balance is kept by one of the greatest perfectionist organisers of crime, Al Capone.

OTHER LITTLE CAPRICORNS

Mums and Dads like you delighted in bringing up the following little achievers. Yours will probably turn out to be even more famous!

First Decanate Capricorn

Nostradamus, Madame de Pompadour, Sir Isaac Newton, Giacomo Puccini, Louis Pasteur, Henri Matisse, Mao Tse Tung, Howard Hughes, Humphrey Bogart, Marlene Dietrich, Quentin Crisp, Little Richard, Anthony Hopkins, Sissy Spacek, Annie Lennox, Henry Miller.

Second Decanate Capricorn

St Bernadette of Lourdes, Francis Poulenc, Simone de Beauvoir, George Balanchine, Gracie Fields, Gerald Durrell, Isaac Asimov, Victor Borge, Richard Nixon, J.R.R. Tolkein, Elvis Presley, Joan Baez, Rod Stewart, Nicolas Cage, Mel Gibson, Diane Keaton, David Bowie, Shirley Bassey.

Third Decanate Capricorn

Joan of Arc, Molière, Benjamin Franklin, Paul Cézanne, Anne Brontë, Albert Schweitzer, Al Capone, A.A.Milne, Mack Sennett, Oliver Hardy, Frederick Fellini, Bebe Daniels, Danny Kaye, Martin Luther King, Janice Joplin, Muhammad Ali, Sade.

AND NOW THE

PARENTS

♈

THE ARIES PARENT

The good news!

The way you look at everything is as a challenge for you to throw every bit of your unlimited Arian energy and supreme self-will into. If you're going to be a parent you're going to outparent all the others and be the best in the world or at least have a great deal of fun trying! Exuberant, with an almost childlike enthusiasm and love of adventure, you may be taken aback by the serious and often grown-up manner of your tiny Capricorn. These little ones like to know what is expected of them and

when, and set about
conscientiously living
up to these standards
to the best of their
abilities. Aries will ad-
mire this youngster's
dogged ambition and
attention to routine de-
tails and be delighted
by the sudden out-

bursts of zany humour that seem so out of
character with the normally serious manner. The
term 'Giddy Goat' must have been made for Capricornians. Anyway it makes a good safety valve
for all that discipline. Aries will see that, despite
Junior's sober ways, this is no stick-in-the-mud
child, and Arian encouragement and enthusiasm
is about all this one needs in order to aim higher
and higher. Although very different in many ways,
you both share a strong sense of ambition. You

approach any challenge with a battle cry, a full frontal attack and the greatest of optimism and unlimited energy, getting up and starting again every time you fall down. Little Capricorn lays down a wealth of good groundwork, approaches each stage in the operation only when the previous one has been successfully completed and takes all the time in the world just to make absolutely sure he gets it right first time. As long as you both understand each other's methods, exasperating as you may sometimes seem to each other, all will be smooth-running.

...and now the bad news!

The main difficulties in this relationship can come with Aries expanding and confining the rules at a moment's notice, leaving Junior confused to say the least. Consistency is security to young Capricorn. In the simplest terms, you want to get things done quickly and well while your little Goat wants to get things done comfortably (in your terms slowly) and well. Working on a shared project can bore you to tears, just waiting for little Capricorn to come to the point that you were at yesterday. Give yourself a break, sit back and watch how thoroughly and conscientiously your little Capricorn applies herself to each task. Maybe a little of this one's sensible preparation could rub off on the impetuous old Ram to your advantage!

THE TAURUS PARENT

The good news!

You love your comforts and the good things of life and will go to great lengths to make sure that your loving family share them with you. The Taurean home is usually the most comfortable and tastefully decorated in the neighbourhood. You're in luck; another of the good things in life has arrived in the guise of little Capricorn. This is a meeting of good, practical, down-to-earth, like minds. The Taurean parent will find few problems and achieve an easy relationship with this conscientious and serious little Capricornian. Both like system and order and are happiest living to an efficient and comfortable routine. Young Capricorn learns steadily and keeps up well with the expected norm at each stage. In good solid Taurean style, you'll never push for speed in preference to thoroughness. This will suit your small helper admirably. The great love of home and family that this couple have in common can find good expression in shared duties around the house. Junior loves to help and feel responsible for little jobs that

show tangible results. Little Goats are sociable and mix well with other children. Though rarely pushy leader types, they establish their place amongst their fellows through their natural talent for organisation. Whenever someone is needed to remember the rules of the game, to pick the best sides and generally keep the game from deteriorating into a typical, all yelling, all fighting, brawl, your little Capricorn will be the other kids' choice. She'll take on the responsibility like she was made for it.

...and now the bad news!

Your love of routine will bring the two of you close together like a smooth-running machine. The trouble is that it can get all too comfortable for either of you to be stimulated into doing anything new or adventurous at all. Too little experiment and imagination can turn young Capricorn into a dull, bossy, 'holier than thou' child, raining 'you shoulds' and 'you oughts' on to less conscientious playmates. Not a good recipe for popularity. These youngsters have a crazy sense of humour; don't let it get buried in all that earthiness. If neither of you like to break the routine and do something spontaneously, then mark in on the schedule for each day of the week a regular space for clowning around and introduce an extra pleasurable bonus into your lives.

THE GEMINI PARENT

The good news!

The happiest days of your life were in childhood, so much so that you've never really left it.
Still managing to see the world through the ever
curious quicksilver mind of the child, you approach
parenthood with a head start. Well, knowing all
there is to know about being a child you're now
going to find out you've got it all wrong. The
Gemini will find the untiring concentration and
dogged devotion to learning of little Capricorn
conflicts strongly with Geminean ideas of carefree

childhood. Often seeming older and more serious than their tender years would suggest, little Goats never falter in their slow, sure steps to independence. From quite early on, responsible little Capricornians begin to insist, in no uncertain terms, that their lives be run to a good predictable routine. There may be times when your little one seems more like a stuck-in-a-rut nine to five worker than a bubbly babe. Variety-loving Geminis may

feel this a bit of a drag but, to Junior, order spells happiness. The bonus is that, if Gemini adapts with a little more system than usual, the resulting independence of Capricorn makes life much easier for both. Gemini's wit and imagination can work wonders in softening this little worker's sometimes too serious outlook. Just a whisker below the surface of this no-nonsense prodigy lies the zaniest sense of fun. Help release it now and again; it's a good safety valve.

...and now the bad news!

Despite all your best intentions, you're just not going to be there, getting it right every time. No consolation that some Geminis you know aren't there getting it right any of the time. You love your freedom to drop plans at the last minute in favour of something much more exciting. Disconcerted by lack of system, unexpected letdowns and sudden changes of plans, Junior will become a crusty critic, nagging disapproval of all and sundry. Keep as near to the pattern as you can and you'll have a delightful paragon of helpfulness. Even put your little one in charge of your busy schedule and ask advice on last-minute changes. Give Capricorn some control and everybody benefits.

THE CANCER PARENT

The good news!

You live life totally through your emotions and
all of your feelings of protectiveness and love are
devoted to your family. Sensitive to the needs of
those around you, you take a pleasure in knowing
just what each and everyone needs to keep everything on an even keel. Little Capricorns want to
go at their own pace within a well-defined set of
guidelines. The Cancerian parent will respond to
this need, showing clearly what is acceptable behaviour and what is not. Although easy-going with

children, Cancer understands that the Capricorn respect for authority provides an example for their own ambitions. Little Goats watch and learn from people they admire in order to climb the heights safely. Both parent and child share a love of the past, well-established tradition and proven methods. If the Cancerian sensitive imagination combines with Capricorn's patient determination they will each benefit.

Capricorns are firmly entrenched in reality and for this reason may miss a great deal of pleasure from more ethereal things. Your sense of fantasy can be greatly helpful in stretching the little Goat's imagination and helping to develop a

more open attitude to less down-to-earth matters. The area which will come easiest is humour and this may well open the door to other things. Both of you will be homebirds, loving the cosiness of just the two of you, being good company for each other. You may have to force yourselves to get out and about, for little Capricorn has to get started on learning the social skills. Learning to mix well with others is more important for little Capricorn, for the real difference between these two signs is that whereas Cancer's life revolves around family, Capricorn's centres on achieving their position in society.

...and now the bad news!

Basically this is an harmonious relationship with little that can go wrong. However, Cancerians are great worriers and have such a vivid (if not sometimes morbid) imagination they are often overprotective to their tiny charges. Little Capricorn, almost totally self-reliant where caution and carefulness is concerned, will see your 'stepping in and taking over' every time things look tricky or difficult for one so young as the insult of all time. Frustrated Goats get bossy, critical and overbearing and you'll have battles on your hands. Stand back and take note that your little Goat rarely gets fingers burned or elbows bruised if left to his own devices. Don't forget a little praise now and again, too. They never ask for it, but it's always welcome.

♌ THE LEO PARENT

The good news!

You're generous to a fault and fill your home with sunshine, love and, above all, pride in your family. The Capricorn child, responsive to good discipline, thrives on a well-ordered upbringing. Leo parents, enjoying great pride in their offspring, will delight in the young Goat's perfect manners and sense of responsibility. Parent and child seek achievement in life, but whereas Leo tends rather to take the world by storm, young Capricorn will work slowly but surely towards a goal. The Leo parent, preferring quick action, may feel that this reserved, plodding youngster needs winding up, the safety switch taken off and a good push-start in the right direction. This rarely works, and hustling – where cautious, careful, little Sea-Goats are concerned – can only produce insecurity. The need to prove themselves by steady achievement conquers the common Capricorn trait, self-doubt. Praise is an important morale booster and no one delivers it as effectively as the confident Leo par-

ent. Although ambitious, little Capricornians never push themselves to the fore, shying away from all forms of show. Often appearing grown-up almost before they are out of rompers, it's all too easy for Leo parents – who love a willing slave – to place too much responsibility, too soon, on these able small shoulders. A little extra help with the fun side of life – easy for playful Leos – can give a better balance to the somewhat serious 'all work and no play' Capricorn.

...and now the bad news!

Just like you, little Capricorn wants to succeed and be appreciated for it. Although showing lots of talent, timing is all important to the little Goat. This, plus the fact that they never like to be pushed unprepared into the public eye, should give out little messages to this enthusiastic and sometimes over-pushy parent. Leo, getting the show on the road at all costs, can find little Capricorn centre stage, unrehearsed and feeling terrible. The biggest Capricorn fear is not coming up to expectations and with a larger than life parent like you this can double the disaster in little Sea-Goat's eyes. Slow down the pace and admire what he can do rather than showing him what he could do if...

THE VIRGO PARENT

The good news!

You see this tatty, untidy old world as a place where you can be of great use putting things to right and making them run more smoothly and efficiently. In short, you're a perfectionist, knowing that by clearing up chaos and mess around you life can become more pleasurable and offer fewer setbacks for those that you love. Here's good news for you, you've got a buddy who shares your philosophy! This is a good harmonious combination of down-to-earth, capable characters with a strong need for material security. The Virgo parent is devoted to the needs of home and family, understanding easily the little Capricornian's love of a good disciplined routine. The small Goat's respect for authority and Virgo's consistency in this area are well matched, giving little cause for clashes. Rarely 'pushy' by nature, little Capricorns can move easily into popularity amongst their small playmates with their exceptional organising abilities. At school, too, this talent could result in responsibilities such as monitor, form captain, etc., and it is easy to see here the importance of good

humour and tolerance in softening any 'bossiness' that may occur. Plenty of practice in the social arts is beneficial, for modest and hard working as little Capricorn undoubtedly is, she intends to make it to the top eventually in her chosen career. This will see her later taking her place as a respected member of society, so you can't start early enough with the social skills.

...and now the bad news!

Mostly you should get on and even the problems with this relationship will be more noticeable to others than to yourselves. As in all combinations of like minds, there is a tendency to overemphasise certain aspects of the respective natures, and with this couple life could get just a little too serious for Junior's own good. This blend of perfectionist and hard-working achiever may become so insular and supercritical as to make relationships outside the family circle difficult. When you find yourselves playing the 'ain't they awful' game with all and sundry outside your little circle, it's time to lighten up. We aren't all perfect beings like you. The introduction of good measures of fun into the routine can build a more tolerant attitude when dealing with us less conscientious souls. Thanks a million!

THE LIBRA PARENT

The good news!

'People...who need people... are the thingiest thingys in the worrrld' – you know how it goes, it's your song, you sing it! Lovely Librans need to relate and want above all else to please their loved ones. Good harmonious relationships mean a lot to easy-going Librans and they'll work hard to keep their children happy and companionable. Little Capricornians like to know where they stand and what is expected of them and do their very best to come up to scratch. This cut and dried approach has great meaning in the life of the ambitious little Goat but may pose a few problems for the Libran parent. Always seeing the other person's point of view rarely makes for hard and fast rules and throwing the decisions back at Junior with 'Whatever you'd like best, dear' may leave a little to be desired in this one's mind. This little one doesn't want to do what she likes best, she wants to do what she is supposed to do. How's she going to be the most admired and respected member of society otherwise!

The Capricornian respect for authority is their way of learning how to deal with their own future potential as organisers. So the egalitarian, harmonious Libran will have to be boss to suit the little

Goat's needs. Within a regular, familiar and well-organised routine these little workers flourish and grow in confidence. However, a modicum of Libran balance will be necessary to keep Junior from becoming lopsidedly materialistic and too serious. Art, pleasure and good fun (Libran affinities) can be inserted into the routine to advantage. Especially the fun. Under that serious little exterior lurks an explosively funny little looney, who'll keep you in fits if you let him out.

...and now the bad news!

The Libran 'don't mind at all giving in for an easy life' habit often gets the better of you. When it does, it'll get the worst of little Capricorn. These conscientious, responsible little workers have problems if it all becomes a little lopsided. If they see weakness in those they want to admire and look up to, they'll turn on their unpleasantly bossy streak in the appropriate direction. Almost as if they want to make you become firmer. Not nice! Capricorns, even the smallest of them, can throw out 'you shoulds' and 'why didn't yous' till the cows come home. If they learn this at home it won't make them popular carried on into the outside world. Be firm...but always friendly!

THE SCORPIO PARENT

The good news!

Supersleuths like you need to know just what makes others tick. Sensitive to the thoughts and feelings of those around them, especially loved ones, Scorpios put their all into encouraging and bringing the best out in them. Little Capricorns are quietly ambitious, respect authority and are usually paragons of orderliness and good manners. The firm but caring Scorpio parent is a tower of strength, in the shadow of which this little one can confidently blossom. Not quickly though. Strong-willed and positive, earthy little Goats, like their namesakes, tread each step up the mountain with steady precision, erring on the side of caution but never making a slip. That's why a good set of house rules is invaluable and even demanded by these conscientious little workers. You may wonder, with the serious little Capricornian, whatever happened to carefree mischie-vous childhood. Don't worry, this one has it later, probably in the 'teens, and certainly in maturity. Work first, play later for these chaps. Look around you and see just how many fifty-year-old Goats seem to be en-tering their second childhood. Scorpio's

good understanding of psychology enables this parent to pick the right time to loosen up and develop the little one's sense of humour. Little and often is the best recipe. This balance, well maintained, will avoid Junior becoming a holier-than-thou, bossy prude, and featuring low in the popularity stakes. Brought safely through initial shyness, little Capricornians' good organising abilities can make them much in demand amongst more scatterbrained playmates.

...and now the bad news!

Scorpios feel things passionately and yet they hold feelings in, seemingly storing them up for the occasional big emotional outburst that could make even moderately strong men tremble. Heaven help your poor little Sea-Goat when this occurs. Not being as endowed with passion or even anything but a modest emotional life, excesses in this area will be embarrassing for your down-to-earth youngster. Little Capricorns need to look up to their role models and if they see behaviour they just couldn't feel comfortable with you're off the list where respect is concerned. Keep the firework explosions away from home and you'll still be number one Superparent!

THE SAGITTARIUS PARENT

The good news!

Life is a constant round of great big adventures for you and parenthood is just going to be another one! The sheer exuberant energy generated by the Sagittarian parent will be accepted but rarely emulated by the cautious Capricorn child. Little Goats, with their love and respect for authority, respond to this parental honesty and openness and learn much, but they continue to hold back their own feelings and ideas until really sure of them. This relationship has the potential for an unusual reversal of roles, with Junior seeming to take life more seriously than this enthusiastic parent. 'Old head on young shoulders' rings true for the little Goats. Junior's precocious self-discipline and conscientiousness relieves Sagittarius from 'heavy parent' duties but will demand in return a strict adherence to good routine. Take away familiar order and system and little Capricorn gets edgy. Same thing, same time every day, seems to work with the necessities anyway. It's a bit of a bore but if your little Goat blossoms then what's to lose? The Sagittarian parent's fund of knowledge and great sense of fun will do much to loosen up the over-serious nature of this youngster. Although

Capricorn, always ambitious, needs little encouragement to 'get on', small, tangible rewards are more appreciated than a wealth of praise. Their own expression of love is more likely to manifest in the same practical way, showing in helpfulness rather than big demonstrations of affection. Love for them is always shown by something material. As with the other Earth signs, it's what you give, not the thought, that counts!

...and now the bad news!

Your love of the truth can get you into trouble often without you knowing it. If you see something wrong you say it, no matter where you are, and no matter who you say it to. Little Capricorns will appreciate the best of your splendid occasional faux pas when the recipient is someone else. However, ambitious little characters that they are, they do not like blunt criticism pointed in their direction. Nevertheless they learn from their 'betters'. Where heavy criticism gets to be the game the Goat can get rough. A fine line has to be drawn not to let loose this less sociable Capricornian talent of falling into the habit of becoming another of the world's great supernags. Smile, Sagittarius, as you open your mouth and put your foot in it. Smile!

THE CAPRICORN PARENT

The good news!

You never take responsibilities lightly, you like
to know where you stand at all times and be absolutely sure that you have a good control over what
is going to happen next in your life. Luck has no
place in your book when you can achieve your aims
with good sense and patient work. Great – you're
in luck! You've just acquired the perfect partner
to share this heavy load. The Capricorn child will
find great support and understanding in the Capricorn parent. These youngsters take life very

seriously in the early years, often not letting up on rigid self-discipline until reaching maturity. You remember, you did it yourself! With this relationship we may find almost a reversal of roles, with the parent youthful and relaxed and the child dutiful and conscientious. The need to, and indeed the love of, patiently applying themselves to the business of learning, will be understood by this parent, and although encouraged, never allowed to become obsessive. The little Capricornian's confidence thrives on order and system, so it will help in relating to other children if you add a little tomfoolery to the schedule. You

should know as well as any that Goats can knock others sideways when it comes to zany humour. Little Capricorn Mack Sennett who invented the Keystone Cops, must have kept his family in fits. Keep the fun side of your relationship regular though, and it'll be more acceptable, for cautious little Goats will find it hard to take unpredictable and unprecedented 'madness' from Mum or Dad. Well-mannered and respectful of authority, these children rarely show their strong ambition in 'pushy' or more aggressive ways. Quietly confident, they pick the right time and the right place to shine.

...and now the bad news!

There'll be few clashes in such a good smooth-running partnership and about the only thing that could go wrong is forgetting the fun. With all that comfortable obedience, parent Goat may overlook the lighter side of this youngster, producing a perfect prig instead of a precious paragon. Although your little one can be trusted to work alone, it's better that you share plenty of relaxing activities. Games concerned with money and time such as Monopoly (could have been invented by a Capricornian), chess etc., making useful but artistic presents for people's birthdays, keeping a diary, patience games (jigsaws, crosswords) and visits to historical places – great fun for little Goats!

The Aquarius Parent

The good news!

You care for your fellow man, woman, and child. You're in this world to right wrongs, overturn injustices and replace outworn traditions that are no longer relevant to society today. Now you've got a real problem – a Capricornian child! Only joking! Aquarians may well qualify as the most easy-going parents around. They like to give their children free rein and encourage their independence and ability to think for themselves. As a rule they're pretty unshockable, though they may very well be surprised that little Capricorn doesn't rush off to take advantage of all that liberty with much enthusiasm. Small Goats actually thrive on a bit of discipline and can feel utterly lost if their parents don't provide a few firm guidelines. All's well if the Aquarian parent understands that this youngster prefers the well-beaten track, only exploring new ground with the utmost caution. However, the free-thinking Aquarian parent can do much to widen the horizons of the sometimes 'blinkered' little

Capricorn. Aquarius is in fact fundamentally concerned with the future, whereas Capricorn clings faithfully to tradition. A meeting of old and new can be enlightening to both parent and child. The stimulating Aquarian household is likely to have much coming and going of interesting and unusual visitors, giving the sometimes shy little Capricornian ample opportunity to gain confidence in dealing with others socially. This will be important later when your youngster takes a responsible position in society. Capricornians are achievers, and they get there by being comfortable and confident in the company of others.

...and now the bad news!

There are bound to be clashes with such a contrasting couple but the little Goat's respect for authority will make this child's reactions less severe, especially if just occasionally the Water

Carrier can slip into a 'traditional' role. The real area where there can be problems though, is in expressing feelings to each other. Both of you shy away from dramatic shows of emotions but in this relationship, where few demands are made in this area, the loss can be little Capricorn's. These small folk need plenty of affection. They are, after all, Earth signs caring more for a loving hug than an 'of course Mummy loves you'.

THE PISCES PARENT

The good news!

You, the sensitive Pisces parent, to whom the world of the imagination is a very real thing, may be gently brought down to earth by the practical nature of the Capricorn child. Tales of pixies and fairies with 'happy ever after' endings so beloved by Pisces in their own childhood may be resisted by the supremely 'sensible' little Goat in favour of Tommy the Tractor and Billy the Bulldozer. To Capricorn, the world of reality is what it's all about. For imaginative Pisces, coming to terms with this youngster will be no chore. The job is to commend the common sense and expand the breadth of vision at the same time. Capricorn children are distinguished by their serious approach and out-standing self-discipline. The phrase 'an old head on young shoulders' was probably coined when someone had met a little Goat. It certainly fits the small Capricornian well. However, those talents aside, Junior may need more than a little help with the fun aspects of living. Piscean whimsy can go a long way in achieving a balance for this youngster,

though spontaneity may have to give way to a regular fun routine: tomfoolery from four to four-thirty each day could make more sense to this Capricorn super-organiser. With you, expression of feelings is immediate: if you're sad you cry, if you're happy you hug everyone in sight. Little Capricorn will never feel comfortable doing the same. Love, for your little Goat, will be expressed in material ways and by helping Mum or Dad. Find plenty of ways that you can both work together in harmony and you will be building a warm and emotionally secure little Capricorn. Even the spontaneous hugs may come in time.

...and now the bad news!

Pisceans care so much about their children and worry about them to such an extent that they can go over-the-top spoiling them. Giving in under pressure is almost unavoidable for an 'old softie'

Piscean. If little Capricorn gets the idea that some-one whom he wants to look up to is weak or unsure of themselves, the respect is lost. Even tiny Goats can become highly critical and bossy without a good strong role model, so don't give in to every whim. Apart from this, clashes will be minimal as long as good guidelines are maintained, and if al-lowed full expression this little one's need to be helpful around the home will make for close and busy companionship.

On the Cusp

Many people whose children are born on the day the sun changes signs are not sure whether they come under one sign or another. Some say one is supposed to be a little bit of each but this is rarely true. Adjoining signs are very different to each other so checking up can make everything clear. The opposite table gives the exact Greenwich Mean Time (GMT) when the sun moves into Capricorn and when it leaves. Subtract or add the hours indicated below for your nearest big city.

AMSTERDAM	GMT + 01.00	MADRID	GMT + 01.00
ATHENS	GMT + 02.00	MELBOURNE	GMT + 10.00
BOMBAY	GMT + 05.30	MONTREAL	GMT - 05.00
CAIRO	GMT + 02.00	NEW YORK	GMT - 05.00
CALGARY	GMT - 07.00	PARIS	GMT + 01.00
CHICAGO	GMT - 06.00	ROME	GMT + 01.00
DURBAN	GMT + 02.00	S.FRANCISCO	GMT - 08.00
GIBRALTAR	GMT + 01.00	SYDNEY	GMT + 10.00
HOUSTON	GMT - 06.00	TOKYO	GMT + 09.00
LONDON	GMT 00.00	WELLINGTON	GMT + 12.00

DATE	ENTERS CAPRICORN	GMT	LEAVES CAPRICORN	GMT
1984/85	DEC 21	4.23 PM	JAN 20	2.58 AM
1985/86	DEC 21	10.08 PM	JAN 20	8.47 AM
1986/87	DEC 22	4.03 AM	JAN 20	2.41 PM
1987/88	DEC 22	9.46 AM	JAN 20	8.25 PM
1988/89	DEC 21	3.28 PM	JAN 20	2.07 AM
1989/90	DEC 21	9.22 PM	JAN 20	8.02 AM
1990/91	DEC 22	3.07 AM	JAN 20	1.47 PM
1991/92	DEC 22	8.54 AM	JAN 20	7.33 PM
1992/93	DEC 21	2.43 PM	JAN 20	1.23 AM
1993/94	DEC 21	8.26 PM	JAN 20	7.08 AM
1994/95	DEC 22	2.23 AM	JAN 20	1.01 PM
1995/96	DEC 22	8.17 AM	JAN 20	6.53 PM
1996/97	DEC 21	2.06 PM	JAN 20	12.43 AM
1997/98	DEC 21	8.07 PM	JAN 20	6.46 AM
1998/99	DEC 22	1.57 AM	JAN 20	12.38 PM
1999/00	DEC 22	7.44 AM	JAN 20	6.23 PM
2000/01	DEC 21	1.38 PM	JAN 20	12.17 AM
2001/02	DEC 21	7.22 PM	JAN 20	6.03 AM
2002/03	DEC 22	1.15 AM	JAN 20	11.53 AM
2003/04	DEC 22	7.04 AM	JAN 20	5.43 PM
2004/05	DEC 21	12.42 PM	JAN 19	11.22 PM

John Astrop is an astrologer and author, has written and illustrated over two hundred books for children, is a little Scorpio married to a little Cancerian artist, has one little Capricorn psychologist, one little Pisces songwriter, one little Virgo traveller and a little Aries rock guitarist. The cats are little Sagittarians.